To my family and friends who live life selflessly.

Contents

Preface

I was born in December of 1963, which meant in October of 2012 I was both 48 years old and I was going to turn 50 "next year". I had celebrated milestone birthdays in the past...when I turned 35 I was preparing for a bodybuilding contest. When I turned 40 I decided to head west to Arizona and try that out for a while. When I turned 45 I ran a half-marathon. I started to think about what I would do for the big 5-0.

One Monday evening that October I was watching football on my Franklin, Tennessee patio with my neighbor, Scott Williams. Scott is a native Tennessean who had been raised in the Memphis area and relocated to Franklin just a year earlier. My wife, Lisa, and I relocated to Franklin from Arizona early in 2012 and over the few months leading up to that October evening Lisa and I had begun to build a strong friendship with Scott and his wife Sharon.

Scott is a likable, outgoing person whose speaking style is very deliberate and very southern. On that October evening when I brought up the fact that I was looking for a challenge to commemorate my 50th, Scott suggested maybe this milestone was significant enough to change things up from past milestone challenges. Scott reminded me that each of my milestone challenges in the past had always really just been focused on me. Scott then challenged me to make this milestone about someone else.

I had gone into my conversation with Scott thinking maybe I'd summit a mountain, or start doing warrior runs, or maybe I'd take up CrossFit. What I was looking for in striking up that conversation was a reason to do something like that. What I came away with was self-reflection and doubt about the life I had led.

If I had been so focused on myself at the major milestones of my life, how selfish had I been during any other year and on any given day? How did others see me? How did my children see me? If it all ended tomorrow, what was my legacy?

There are times in all of our lives where a moment defines us. There are few times, for most of us, where we define the moment. I now had the opportunity for this to be one of those times...and I had no idea what to do or where to start.

Chapter 1 – The Social Ingredient

Americans love to debate about seemingly countless topics and Social Media is just one of them. Many people see Social Media services as invasive and a waste of time. Others find them to be a lifeline to a network of people they have connected with in business and in their personal lives. One irony of the Social Network debate is the number of people who utilize Social Networking as a tool to facilitate those debates.

I am in the camp that finds two Social Networking tools to be particularly useful for me. I leverage LinkedIn (175 million users at the time of this writing) for Social Networking on a business level. LinkedIn tells me that I have 276 "connections" and that those connections link me to over 15 million people. There are a lot of people who "connect" with virtually every person they meet, whether that be at work, on a cruise, at a conference, or in their neighborhood fitness center. These people typically have hundreds and hundreds of connections and achieve the status of LinkedIn Lion. I have typically handled LinkedIn a little more conservatively. I have always felt that I should understand who you are and what you are about in order for us to "connect". I have to feel a certain level of trust in order for my name to show up on your connections list, and vice versa.

I treat Facebook (over 1 billion active users at the time of this writing) very much the same way as LinkedIn. If we are friends in life, then we can be "Friends" in

Facebook. If we don't know much about each other it is unlikely that I am going to either send or accept a "Friend" request from you.

Many of my Facebook Friends are connections that I made in high school or during the time I served in The United States Marine Corps. Facebook has helped me reconnect with some friends that I have literally not seen in 30 years or more. I have watched their children grow up and I am even starting to see their children's children grown up. I am able to see and share in some of the most exciting events of their lives and, sadly, in some of the most traumatic events of their lives.

One of my friends on Facebook is Barb. Barb and I went to high school together back in the late 1970s. I remember Barb being very likable in high school. When we reconnected on Facebook I was able to see that Barb is now a delivery room nurse and that she loves her job. Being a nurse her work schedule sometimes requires her to work weekends and holidays. Instead of complaining about missing time with her family and friends while she works, Barb posts comments about her experiences as she helps doctors and parents bring new life into the world. It's rare that any post from Barb doesn't contain words like "love", "hope" or "joy". My morning routine regularly starts with a cup of coffee and a review of the news, ESPN, Facebook and LinkedIn. My day always gets an early shot in the arm when Barb has been busy posting.

One morning late in 2012 I launched Facebook and found condolences and prayers being directed to Barb and her family. The news wasn't good. Barb's brother had died as the result of a tragic accident at work. Barb was devastated and the bright light that led so many of us into each day went dark.

When Barb did venture back out onto Facebook she shared the link to a song that she had been listening to as she coped with her brother's passing. The song was inspirational and gave hope that the world her lost loved one had ascended to was far better than anything the rest of us could imagine.

I mentioned earlier that I live in Franklin, TN. Franklin is a very popular town for country music's singers, musicians and songwriters. I have met a couple of songwriters that are members of the golf club I joined when we moved here. Just a couple of months before Barb's loss I was introduced to the songwriter who co-wrote the inspirational song that Barb posted on Facebook.

At first I really didn't know how to reach out to Barb on the topic. What I did know was that she still wasn't back to being herself. I also knew that the song she had posted, and the comments she had included with that post, gave her hope that her brother was in a better place.

Through a mutual friend I was able to contact the songwriter and share the story of Barb's loss. He told me he was going to leave something for me to send to Barb, and that I could pick it up at the clubhouse. A few days later I showed up at the club for a Sunday afternoon round of golf and there was a package for me behind the counter. In the package was a small, hardcover book written by the songwriters. The book, based on the song Barb had posted online, included words of encouragement, hope, faith and inspiration. There was also a CD of the single in the back cover.

I took the book home and immediately sat at the kitchen table and read each page. After doing so I was convinced that this might help Barb to heal. I took out a piece of paper and wrote Barb a note, telling her I was sorry for her loss and that I hoped that time was helping to heal her grieving heart. The hand-written note was key for me...this was a personal matter for Barb and I wanted her to have the privacy she needed as she grieved over her loss.

I am sharing this story because of what happened next. When Barb received the package containing the book, CD and letter she immediately posted about it on Facebook. Barb was so happy, and surprised, that someone that she had not seen or spoken to in 30 years would go out of their way to commit such a gesture on her behalf. Over the next several days the number of comments and "Likes" added to her post mounted. I felt conflicted as I read those comments and reviewed the number of "Likes". Barb was back to being the light that inspired others and that was awesome, but at the same time, some of the attention being given in those "Comments" was directed at me, and that was not my intention at all. Don't get me wrong, it warmed my heart to see the responses and to see how many people appreciated my gesture. That said, I had intended for this Act of Kindness to be personal and now it had become very public. For days, as I reflected over the entire event, I wondered if I should have sent the book to Barb anonymously.

It is hard to explain, but doing something kind for someone else makes you feel good in the process. Feeling good about it makes it almost feel like a selfish gesture. Doing something that is selfish is not something you want others to know about and, therefore, not something that you want to show up on Facebook. This psychological conflict is important to remember as I tell the story of 1,000 Selfless Acts.

Chapter 2 – The Reach

For most of my career I have preferred to work for small companies, but at this stage in my life I have become less-interested in the "razor's edge" of profitability and more interested in the security provided by a larger employer. Now I work for a very large Fortune 500 company and, as you either know or can imagine, that comes with its benefits and challenges.

One of the benefits of being an employee of the company I work for is the training. While many companies attempt to create knowledge- and career-management systems and resources, my employer has done it. One of the programs offered to employees includes recorded senior-level-management-session presentations that are posted for every employee to be able to access electronically. This program runs throughout the year and there is, on average, one video posted for each month of the year.

In 2012, my first year with the company, I watched all of the leadership session videos that were posted. One such session featured a guest presenter named Eric Weihenmayer. Eric is a blind adventurist who skydives, kayaks through dangerous river rapids and, most notably, is the first blind person to have summited Mt. Everest as well as the highest peak on each of the seven continents.

Early in his life Eric was diagnosed with a disease that would one day take his eyesight. Having received his diagnosis as a child Eric had a lot of time to consider the implications of, one day, being blind. Time and again in his presentations Eric says that he was not afraid of being blind as much he was afraid of being swept off to the side for the rest of his life. Eric eventually went blind in his early teen years and it was only after becoming blind that he decided to take up climbing.

In his presentations, Eric talks in detail about "the reach", or extending yourself beyond what you can "see" to find that next foothold or handhold in order to continue your ascent. He metaphorically talks about "the reach" and how those who have the courage to stretch themselves beyond what is comfortable are the ones who reach summits that those who do not take on that risk will never achieve.

Eric gives examples of disabled people who scale and climb some of the world's most famous rock formations and mountains, using innovation, determination and "the reach". He talks about those who harness the energy of adversity and use it as a fuel rather than letting adversity create a barrier or burden that prevents achievement. Eric refers to those who can leverage adversity as alchemists and says they are the people who can "turn lead into gold".

Eric's presentation was inspiring, uplifting and motivating, but he cautioned that in order to do great things you have to expect adversity. Having seen his presentation and knowing that I wanted to do something for others, I braced myself for the adversity that was sure to come my way. I began to imagine what form adversity would take and I imagined ways to harness that adversity to fuel my objective.

To end his presentation, Eric quoted Helen Kellar when he said *"I am only one, but still I am one. I cannot do everything, but still I can do something; and because I cannot do everything, I will not refuse to do something that I can do"*. That quote has had a clear and visible impact on me since I heard it and it was certain to fuel my actions when it came to my 50th birthday challenge.

Chapter 3 – The Thought Provokers

Armed with the objective to do something different for my 50th birthday, and challenged by Scott to do it for others, I reached out to a few friends for clarity.

Will Kirchoffer has been a friend of mine for almost 30 years. Will and I were stationed together in the Marines a couple of times...once back in 1983 down in Albany, Georgia and once again in 1985 in Okinawa Japan. Since our time together in the service, and mostly because of Will's persistence, we have stayed in touch. Will is literally one of those rare people you meet that, once you become his friend, you are his friend for life. When he does contact me I typically take a fair amount of ribbing from him because he had to initiate that contact yet again.

Will reached out to me around Thanksgiving 2012 to catch up on our lives, our families, jobs, etc. At some point in the conversation I told Will about my quest to find a meaningful way to help others around my 50th birthday. Will, probably not surprisingly, suggested that maybe I do something to help the "Wounded Warriors", an organization focused on helping service members who incurred a physical or mental injury, illness, or wound, co-incident to their military service on or after September 11, 2001 and their families. We talked about it for a few minutes, talked a little more about our families, our mutual friends and our holiday plans, and then we said our goodbyes.

I then reached out to another of my dear friends, Glenn Mathis. Glenn and I had worked together for 8 years, but we had really developed a brother-like friendship over the last 5 years. Glenn and I talked about the challenge, Eric Weihenmayer and the inspiration he'd given me, and Will's suggestion to focus on the Wounded Warriors. Glenn then passionately spoke about the need for stronger anti-bullying awareness and programs. He talked about physical, psychological and cyber bullying and cited a couple of examples where young people had taken their own lives as a result of being bullied. My niece, Steph Cole, had just completed a Social Networking project around anti-bullying where she worked to raise awareness using Facebook as a vehicle to share information. I told Glenn about her efforts and how my personal awareness had been impacted by her work. As with my conversation with Will, Glenn and I talked about it for a few minutes and said our goodbyes.

Oddly enough these two conversations and the example set by my niece started to form an idea for my challenge. I began to think that I could probably go to 1,000 different people and find nearly as many causes that are near and dear to each person I'd speak with. I started to think maybe my challenge was more than what even Scott had intended in the first place.

Maybe my challenge was to do for other people and in the process to recruit other people to do nice things for even more people. If 1,000 different people would have 1,000 different causes that were important to each of them, then why not see if I could get them to go out and do something about it.

I thought, again, about my niece and how she leveraged Facebook to communicate about anti-bullying. The idea of what to do about my challenge was quickly becoming an action plan I could execute.

The next evening was Wednesday November 21, the day before Thanksgiving, Lisa and I met our friends Larry and Tracy for dinner in downtown Nashville. Larry and Tracy were in town from Atlanta to celebrate the holiday and to visit with Tracy's family.

We parked the car in a paid lot and walked a couple of blocks to the restaurant. It was a crisp evening and you could feel winter, and the holidays, in the air. After we sat down and got caught up I told them I had an idea to cause 1,000 good things to happen for others over the holidays. I told them I thought Facebook would be a good vehicle to issue a challenge to my Facebook Friends and that I'd like each of their feedback on the idea over dinner.

This just happened to be the first time Lisa had heard about this and she cautioned that "1,000 was probably too big of a number"...that maybe I should start with a smaller objective. I reasoned that I'd need my "Friends" help to recruit their "Friends", and so on, but that I thought we could get there and that 1,000 was a strong enough number for people to get behind the effort.

Lisa, Tracy and Larry then all agreed that they thought it could be done and they all committed to helping me out.

At this point I really did not know what to expect, but I did think this kind of challenge could be something special. I thought about "the reach" and I reasoned that this was worth the risk of the unknown.

I also knew that I was going to have to get out in front and lead this challenge. Throughout my life, whether at work, at home or on playing fields, I have always been pretty effective at building consensus and motivating others when I want to get something done. I was sure that people would buy in initially, but I was also concerned that it would get old quickly for some of those who agreed to join forces with me early on. The group was going to have to grow almost daily if we were going to keep the momentum of the challenge moving forward. That meant I was going to need to repeat things almost daily to orient the new recruits. I was going to have to be patient and I hoped that other members of the group would be understanding and exercise patience too.

The worst thing that could happen, I surmised, was that I'd give this a shot and we'd come up short of 1,000 Selfless Acts. Missing the goal would definitely be disappointing, but I felt we'd do a lot of good on our way to failing, if we were going to fail at all.

I weighed all of these things one last time and decided I was up for the challenge, that I'd give it my best, and that I'd probably learn a lot along the way.

Chapter 4 – The Challenge

"Everybody can be great. Because anybody can serve. You don't have to have a college degree to serve. You don't have to make your subject and your verb agree to serve.... You don't have to know the second theory of thermodynamics in physics to serve. You only need a heart full of grace. A soul generated by love." – Dr. Martin Luther King, Jr.

By Thanksgiving Day 2012 the objective to do for others had become clear to me. I posted the following message on Facebook for my Friends to read:

"If you could help me generate 1,000 Selfless Acts by 1/1/2013 would you?"

I then instructed them to simply click "Like" if they wanted to help me out.

After I posted this I sat back and nervously waited for responses. I wasn't so nervous about the potential impact a lack of interest would have on my project, but I was very nervous about what that lack of interest would say about people and the world we live in. I didn't have to wait long to find out.

27 of my Facebook friends read my post and clicked "Like". This gave me hope that an objective like 1,000 Selfless Acts in 39 days was possible. If the group were limited to just those 27, plus me, we would each have to average 36 Selfless Acts a day to reach 1,000. But,

if each of them would follow suit and invite their friends, and in the process were each able to recruit 27 others, the group could potentially be 756 members strong. In hindsight this was probably a lofty goal, but it was possible.

I created a "Group" in Facebook called 1,000 Selfless Acts. I set the permissions on the group so that anyone in the group could invite new members and anyone could post to the group. On the day after Thanksgiving 2012 I added a file to the group that shared some of the context of the challenge already covered in this book. I also added some examples that members of the group could follow, and gave instructions on how we would record the Selfless Acts committed. Here's an excerpt from the file:

"I'd like to share some examples of what I have seen, heard and what I personally have either done or intend to do:

My niece, Stephanie, took on a task of raising Anti-Bullying awareness. Not only is this a very important topic, but most of us only remember the physical bullying that took place when we were kids. We can't imagine how relentless bullying becomes when you mix physical bullying with cyber-bullying. For a month she dedicated her Facebook posts to raising anti-bullying awareness. When I reached out to my good friend, Glenn Mathis, and shared my 1,000 Selfless Acts challenge with him, he immediately talked about anti-bullying and how we need to work together to raise awareness and stop bullying wherever we can.

My friend, Will, suggested helping the Wounded Warrior Project, either financially or as a volunteer.

My friend, Barb, pays it forward every day of her life. As a delivery room Nurse she sees new lives beginning every day she works. She shares some of the most uplifting stories with her friends on Facebook...those stories make my day better every time I read them.

I was sitting on the toll road in Atlanta and the person in front of me paid my toll for me...it was simple and cost them $.50, but it made my day.

My brother talked about how frustrated he was sitting behind a woman "who was apparently in no hurry to get anywhere that morning" in the drive-thru at Starbucks. When he finally did get to the window, the woman he had been frustrated with just 2 mins earlier had already paid for his coffee. That made his day and made him think about his attitude the next time things didn't fit exactly into his schedule.

When someone in the neighborhood gets sick or has surgery, my wife makes their family dinner. It doesn't cost much, but it is a priceless gesture.

I have a bunch of old coats and jackets I hang on to but really will probably never wear much. I am personally going down to an area in downtown Nashville where homeless people hang out, and I am going to literally pull the coats off my back and give them to folks who can really use them.

Every time I walk into a grocery store I grab one stray cart from the parking lot for me to use and one stray cart to just put where it belongs. It saves the store from paying more to run their business, from charging me more to cover that cost, and it might save someone from getting a nice new door ding on their car.

I make it a habit to pick up loose trash folks drop on a parking lot or sidewalk. What's it hurt...the place looks better and maybe someone else sees that example and, before you know it, we've really cleaned things up.

I have 160 friends on Facebook. I have over 250 connections in LinkedIn. LinkedIn says my 278 connections link me to a network of over 15 million people. Facebook has more members than LinkedIn does. My 160 Facebook friends probably link me to over 20 million people. I have to believe that with my friends, your friends and your friends' friends we can easily do and track over 1,000 Selfless Acts that might not have otherwise been done. Feel free to copy my challenge to your Facebook Status and make it your own...I really don't care how we get the message out. I am most interested in creating our own brand of viral kindness that makes the lives of those in our path a little better this holiday season.

If you do have friends who want to join us you can also simply add them to the 1,000 Selfless Acts Facebook Group.

As for sharing the status of Selfless Acts you've done...you can either share exactly what you did (a great way for others to get ideas of what to do), or you can just put a number in a status to the group of how many Selfless Acts you did. For instance, if you just did one, you can simple post "1" or "one". If you want to save up a few and not post every day you can post "5".

I'll count everything up and provide a status/count a couple of times each week.

So, that's the essence of this challenge. Hopefully this information has helped you to understand the goal. If, after having read this, you decide you'd like to opt out, just unlike the post you previously liked. I'll take you off of the group."

We were off and running. Now it was really a matter of who would actively participate, how much people would be willing to share, and how many people would ultimately join the group.

Chapter 5 – The Connectors

A few years ago I read a book called "The Tipping Point" by Malcolm Gladwell. In the book the author wrote of different examples where an initiative or objective hit an inflection point and took off. Mr. Gladwell researched and analyzed several examples where growth and momentum only really took off when "Connectors" got involved. Connectors were those people who become a sort of glue. They are those people that tend to meet and be introduced to a lot of people. Connectors then put people together who can help one another toward an objective or goal.

I read "The Tipping Point" and was fascinated by the examples shared in the book. I suspect that many people who read it tried to figure out how they could create a tipping point in their own business and see the remarkable success that some of the case studies achieved in the book. The author did warn though that there wasn't really a formula to go out and create a tipping point yourself…some initiatives benefitted from a tipping point while others simply did not.

As it relates to 1,000 Selfless Acts I was not even considering a tipping point. I felt like our challenge was going to be the kind of effort that you grind at every single day. I had it in my head that we'd simply need to be at an average number of Selfless Acts every day and that if we got behind we just might not hit our goal. It is much easier to have a great start and give yourself a little room for potential setbacks down the road than it is to try to make up for a slow start.

Over the first few days of the challenge the Selfless Acts trickled in. This was probably the combination of the group launching on Thanksgiving weekend, the start-up size of the group, and members of the group initially being reluctant to post.

Until a Facebook group gets to a certain size (I think it is 100 members) the administrator can see which of the members are viewing the content posted, even if those members are not actively posting themselves. As the Selfless Acts trickled in I could see a lot of people who had been invited to the group were reading what others were doing, but not posting any Selfless Acts themselves.

The fact that members of the group were reluctant to post was, ultimately, a key challenge to the group's success throughout. For me to ask like-minded, generous people to publicly draw attention to their Acts of Kindness was a tough thing to do. There is the feeling that you, just by asking, are a hypocrite of sorts. The same applied to the members of the group. If it were a Selfless Act or an Act of Kindness then the person doing it shouldn't draw attention to her or himself in the process.

I hoped the members of the group would get beyond their apprehension quickly. It was throttling our progress at 25 Selfless Acts a day and that kind of production just wasn't going to get us to our goal. We desperately needed an inflection point. Either those who were sitting on the sidelines were going to need to get in the game or we were going to have to add new members and we needed to add them quickly.

And that's when the Connectors showed up!

In two days the group grew from 110 members to 229, then from 229 to 650. Over a 12-day period the group grew to 1,307 members with 472 of them actively participating. I wasn't sure what constitutes an outbreak, but our little group was growing dramatically and viral kindness was off and running.

I shared the following status report with the group:

Selfless Acts Administrator Post

"162 Selfless Acts total. 62 Selfless Acts posted today alone. This time last night there were 229 people invited and the running total, as of tonight, is 650 invited. This was a BIG day. That said, this whole thing is about much more than the numbers...I can only imagine how some of the people feel who have been on the receiving end of our collective efforts."

Over the next 12 days, the stories and number of Selfless Acts poured in. On December 12, 2012 we eclipsed 1,000 documented Selfless Acts.

Throughout the challenge we were motivated, uplifted, inspired and, more than once, moved to tears by the details the members of the group posted. Members posted about helping children, the elderly, the homeless, our military servicemen and women, animals, victims of tragedy, those with illness, and others in-need over the holidays. People posted about paying for the person's coffee in line behind them, letting someone with less merchandise go before them in the checkout lane, or picking up the toll for the car behind them at a toll booth.

It took us 18 days total to reach our objective. My guess is that our efforts probably resulted in tens of thousands of Acts of Kindness and Good Deeds, as people in the group privately went out of their way to do good, and as those on the receiving end of our Acts of Kindness began to follow the example we'd set.

Over a two-month period leading up to the 1,000 Selfless Acts challenge the news was focused on a polarized America that debated the Presidential Election, big government and the Fiscal Cliff. It focused on Hurricane Sandy and how the super storm had devastated the northeastern United States, leaving millions without power and/or without a home. It focused on an unstable economy and how all of the above could drag America back into a recession.

Tragically, just days after we eclipsed 1,000 Selfless Acts, a lone gunman entered a Connecticut elementary school and killed 26 people, many of them children between the ages of 4 and 6. A lot of Americans felt much like we did after September 11, 2001. We struggled to fall asleep that night and when we woke up the next day we hoped it was just a bad dream. We learned the horrible details of the event, and for days the news was about the heart-wrenching stories created by the tragedy. It seemed that, just like in September 2001, we all had far more questions than answers. Our once vibrant Facebook group went quiet as the world tried to make sense of it all.

After a couple of days people began to talk and to post again. We also began to hear of a movement started by a popular news personality where she challenged every person to do 26 Acts of Kindness in memory of the victims of the school shooting in Connecticut. People all over the world began to post on Twitter the Acts of Kindness and Good Deeds they had committed. The national evening news reported hundreds of thousands of Acts of Kindness being done.

Through unspeakable evil, natural disaster and our seemingly irreconcilable differences, Americans had once again come together like only Americans can do.

Kindness had gone viral, and hope had a fighting chance!

Chapter 6 – Perspective Spotlight

In Chapter 9 you'll have the opportunity to read through many of the Selfless Acts our group committed. In doing so you will likely see comments that changed the group member's perspective who posted the Selfless Act and you may also have your perspective changed in the process.

I made one of the posts regarding the homeless and my perspective. Our perspectives are likely shaped over time by what we see, hear and read as much if not more than by what we experience. My perspective on homeless people changed in a day and I wanted to share it with the group:

Selfless Acts Member Post

"When I was first sharing the concept of 1,000 Selfless Acts I talked about helping the homeless. On the day 1,000 Selfless Acts began I spoke to a person about the challenge and suggested that I'd like to see us help the homeless during the challenge. He commented that he had seen a "60 Minutes" episode (or a similar program) where someone who regularly begged for money on the street as a homeless person was making $65,000 a year and driving a Cadillac. My only thought, and subsequent comment, was that "we can't really apply that thinking across the entire homeless community…no more than we can say that everyone who owns a firearm is going to shoot someone". I get it…a lot of the people who do ask for money are either scamming you or are going to use the money you give them to feed one of their addictions.

If there were only a way to know what your money and your kindness are really going to pay for.

I visited Middle Tennessee in Dec '11 to look for a place to live. While we were driving from house to house, my realtor pointed out the homeless people selling newspapers (referred to as "vendors") at the major intersections. She said the monthly publication is focused on the homeless and that most of the content is written by the homeless themselves.

Several cities in America have similar "street papers" and there are a variety of ways that these papers operate. In Nashville, the street paper is called The Contributor and it serves both the homeless AS WELL AS THE FORMER homeless who have used the paper to build enough of an income that they can afford a very modest roof over their heads. The vendors have to "earn" an ID badge, have to be presentable and sober to keep the badge, and they have to pay for the papers they sell.

Until recently, and only occasionally, I would buy a paper and if I read it at all I would just browse through it.

Leading up to yesterday, and after a pretty busy ~10 days or so, I started to feel like I wasn't pulling my weight around 1,000 Selfless Acts. I've seen so many posts lately where people were investing themselves beyond some of the more-simple Pay it Forward examples we've seen. Don't get me wrong, I think those simple gestures are incredibly important to our cause, but some of the other work folks are doing is really incredible stuff.

So, with my "guilt" building up, I woke up yesterday morning and read three posts that literally changed my day.

1). Kymberly posted that on Saturday she'd gone to the Community Kitchen and fed the homeless and then stopped and gave blood on her way home.

2). Tamara posted about giving the homeless man a coat that she was going to donate to Goodwill. She posted about how nice it was to talk as they walked together to her car so he could pick out the coat he wanted.

3). Ronda bought a homeless person a cup of coffee.

After reading those posts I reorganized my plans for yesterday. I set out to spend my afternoon looking for Selfless Acts that could be done. I put a handful of dollar bills in my cup holder and put a couple of umbrellas on the passenger seat of my SUV. I then headed to the busy intersection in my town where The Contributor vendors can be found selling their papers.

The vendors stand in the grass medians next to the left-hand turn lanes and you almost have to catch a red light in order to buy a paper. From a distance, as I approached the intersection, I started watching the traffic light cycle through. I manipulated my speed and the lane I was in enough to catch the light turning from green to yellow to red without impacting the traffic behind me too much.

The lady selling the paper at this intersection was focused on the task at hand. Her clothes were a little dated, but she was very presentable. I rolled my window down, asked "how much for a paper?" She said the paper was a dollar so I handed her one. She gave me a paper and thanked me. I asked if she needed any water and if she had an umbrella in case the forecasted rain started to fall. She thanked me again and told me she was "all set". The light changed and I moved on.

Because of the configuration of this particular intersection, going around the block is about a 3-mile drive. The intersection is right off of the interstate and there just happens to be a busy shopping mall right there, so you can't really just cut through a parking lot in order to catch a different vendor. I made the loop and caught the light just as it turned red. I motioned for the vendor, this time an older gentleman, to come to the car. I asked "how much for a paper" and he also told me it was a dollar. Again I paid for the paper and asked if he needed any water or an umbrella. Again, the vendor told me he was "all set". I asked him his name and he pointed to his badge and said "Brian". He told me he was a celebrity and that he'd just been on CNN protesting a cause at the courthouse. About that time the light changed and he thanked me again and wished me a great day.

When I got home later that afternoon I grabbed the papers I had bought and brought them in the house. I figured I'd read one and then decide who I would give the papers to when I had finished reading them. I read every word of every article. There were headline articles, an article about a boxer fighting against homelessness, a vendor (person who sells the paper) spotlight, a sports page, 14 poems...even Hoboscopes.

So this is where I found the specific perspective I mentioned yesterday and way back at the beginning of this post.

I read one article called One Step Away. The article was written by a homeless woman who, two years ago, was able to get a seasonal job with Dell doing shipping work. During her time at Dell her mother was diagnosed with lung cancer, yet she continued to work without missing a day. After the holidays had passed she was kept on at Dell as a permanent employee. Within two days she lost her mother and her appendix ruptured. She worked hard to recover and worked harder than ever when she got back to work. At her one-year mark with Dell she was laid off. She looked for work and, in a tough economy, couldn't find it. When her money ran out she lost her "room" and was homeless again.

My Perspective Gained: I wonder how many of those who were homeless and clawed their way out of it are one step away from being homeless again. How many of the homeless have emerged from it only to fall on hard times and find themselves right back in tent city?

I read another article where one of the vendors was interviewed by the newspaper. I won't go into the entire article, but what I do want you to know is that as a 5-yr old child the vendor lost his mother when she was killed in a car accident. His step-father was given custody of him and the child was beaten regularly. He and his step father lived in a rural area and their closest neighbor was a school bus driver who lived a good ways down the dirt road from the boy.

One night he ran away while his step father was away. He banged on the school bus driver's door until it opened. He frantically explained that he needed help and the school bus driver took him in and called 911. He was 8-years old at the time and didn't even weigh 30 lbs.

The child stayed with the bus driver and his wife for the weekend. The bus driver's wife fed him whatever he wanted and he thinks he ate 9 Peanut Butter and Jelly sandwiches, with milk (he pointed out), that first night.

The authorities took him away from his step-father and he spent a year with his foster parents before the adoption paperwork went through that gave his grandparents custody.

As a young adult he struggled with anger and alcoholism and wound up in jail and then homeless.

He is now married and works selling these street papers. He said the biggest thing he has learned is that the past is past and you really can't lay blame. He leans on his faith and he says he has learned to pay forward the breaks he has gotten in life.

My Perspective Gained: Until today I saw a lot of homeless people. To be honest a lot of times I was uncomfortable being around them. I never once, not once, considered how they ended up there. I will never think that way again."

Chapter 7 – Amazing Grace Spotlight

One particular challenge that administering and leading this group presented was to not draw more attention to any one Selfless Act posted. I didn't really have to regularly remind myself that all of the Selfless Acts being committed were worthy, but every once in a while one of the members would post something that sort of stopped each of us in our tracks when we read it.

One such post happened about half-way through the challenge when a school teacher posted a remarkable Act of Kindness she committed on behalf of one of her students. This particular post drew more "Likes" (a lot more) from fellow group members than any other post throughout the challenge.

I am sure that every adult generation has looked back at the generations making their way up and wondered how they will do at shouldering the load when we turn the world over to them. We all play a part in developing and grooming the young so that when the time comes their generation will be ready. Parents, grandparents, teachers and coaches are all responsible for molding children into young men and women who eventually become husbands, wives, parents, business professionals and political leaders themselves.

As adults we all draw on the lessons we learned and examples we learned from while growing up. Some elicit memories so powerful that we remember almost every detail about the day the moment took place...whether it was clear or cloudy, warm or cold; whether the event happened early in the morning or late in the day.

I suspect that this Act of Kindness has already created a memory and set an example for this young person that she will remember for the rest of her life.

Selfless Acts Member Post

"There's a girl at the high school where I teach and her family doesn't have much money. She is a sweet girl, but she gets made fun of by the other girls because she is overweight and doesn't have many clothes that fit her. She often comes to school in old sweat pants and tee shirts.

I went through my closets last night to find any clothes that I might have to pass on to her that don't fit me anymore. I found a sack full of clothes I had forgotten about that were just about her size. They all still had the price tags on them and had never been worn. They were like new.

I ended up taking her 2 pairs of jeans and 5 very nice winter tops and jackets. I told her a friend of mine had a daughter her age and size and didn't want them. (This saved her from thinking she's getting 'teacher' clothes)

She was so excited! Just seeing the look on her face was the best Christmas present ever."

When I read this post I literally felt my breath being taken away. For what felt like an hour I sat speechless and re-read the post several times.

When I decided to write about the 1,000 Selfless Acts challenge I tried to think of the most succinct way to express this teacher's actions. If you look up the synonyms for the word "grace" you'll find, among others, elegance, refinement, loveliness, style, poise and charm. In my humble opinion this Selfless Act was all of the above and more.

Chapter 8 – Love and Loss Spotlight

Every 1,000 Selfless Acts post gave the person posting the opportunity to share what they had done. I think just as importantly it gave them, as well as those who responded to the post with a comment, the opportunity to share what they were feeling.

During the challenge members would post to the group and ask if what they had done constituted a Selfless Act. Because of my role as leader of the group it seemed that our members looked to me to be the ultimate authority on what counted and what did not.

Members wanted to know, early on, if doing something for a family member counted, if picking up trash counted, or if putting away a neighbor's garbage can counted. In one case, and you'll have the opportunity later on to read the post, a member doubted whether saving someone's life on a commercial airline flight was a Selfless Act or just something he was supposed to do.

I tried to convey the general rule that if you went out of your way to do something for others, or if you did something on behalf of someone else that you could have otherwise not done, that it probably counted as a Selfless Act. I also let the members know that they knew better than anyone if the act the committed was worthy of being counted as a Selfless Act.

One member of the group asked if by helping her best friend through her terminally ill mother's last days would count as a Selfless Act. By now I suspect that you have a pretty good idea of the contrast that the author of this book and administrator of 1,000 Selfless Acts presents. Yes, I am a 9-year Veteran of the USMC; yes, I am a business professional who has had to make tough decisions that have adversely impacted employee's livelihoods; and, yes, I am a sensitive person who tends to feel a great deal of empathy for all living things.

So, when this group member looked to me to be the authority on whether her taking care of her friend who was preparing to lose her mother constituted a Selfless Act or not, I literally had to fight through the tears to tell her that it "absolutely" counted. I asked her to consider the alternative to being there when her friend needed her the most. Imagine sitting on the sideline and not helping to shoulder that immense pain.

I remember a friend once telling me that "as young people we tend to focus on ourselves and we do what we want to do, but eventually we grow up and start doing what we are supposed to do". The responsibility of being a true friend often challenges us to do what we are supposed to do, regardless of the pain we have to endure in the process.

Over multiple posts we witnessed a love for a friend that we all could be so lucky to ever find. I am so very proud to be able to share this post with you here.

Selfless Acts Member Post

"Sat next to my best friend, hand in hand for 12+ hrs on Tuesday, while her mother passed away, losing a battle with Lung Cancer. The hospice team couldn't believe the support and love that was in the room that day. There were 7 of us in total including Andree (the woman who passed). Over the course of 5 days we all took turns being there, bringing clothes, food (and wine) and love. We said prayers, we laughed, we cried, we ordered pizza, we went through a LOT of tissues. We stayed together. Tuesday night, after Andree passed, I drove Martine's car home so she could ride with her sister. When I got to her house I realized there was medical equipment everywhere and so I cleaned up as quickly as I could to make it feel more 'normal' (if that is even possible after losing your mother who lived with you) .... put all the hospital stuff away and found some wine and crackers. More friends rallied and we all sat for a couple hours with Martine and reminisced about the wonderful life her mother lead and how many people she touched in her short 70 years. These Selfless Acts we are all doing ... it's important. People matter. Not money, not jobs, not the clothes we wear or the cars we drive. People."

Chapter 9 – The Acts

I hope you enjoy the following examples of the collective good that a group of strangers did in less than three weeks. I hope you are inspired and motivated...that you become more mindful of your surroundings, and that you yourself might go out of your way to do something for someone else that you might not have otherwise done. I also hope that you regularly find yourself on the receiving end of Selfless Acts and that the warm feeling you get from getting will help sustain your own desire to give.

Seeing is Believing

"Helping, fixing and serving represent three different ways of seeing life. When you help, you see life as weak. When you fix, you see life as broken. When you serve, you see life as whole. Fixing and helping may be the work of the ego, and service the work of the soul." – Rachel Naomi Remen

Selfless Acts Member Post

In thinking about this challenge, I really think it is as much about raising the level of consciousness within me. Be more aware of how I act, what I do, etc. and in doing so I think I will be more open to what I can do to be a more productive person in my life and for those around me. This isn't changing anyone's life but in an effort to raise my level of consciousness, I made a point of really seeing people today. Everywhere I went, BestBuy, Target, dinner, I made a point of being attentive to those that I normally am not too focused on…the waitress, the cashiers, the people in the store. I just made sure to thank them all, asked how they were and meant it. Not much, but I am ashamed it made me realize I have not been very good lately of being aware of the people around me that I don't know…recognizing them instead of seeing through them. Think I'll do it tomorrow too.

Selfless Acts Member Post

This is a small one, but still a little difficult since it violates Chicago's folkways. I looked each person I passed at the train station in the eye and wished them a great day.

Selfless Acts Member Post

Complimented a complete stranger and made them smile.

Selfless Acts Member Post

I was in line at the grocery store, the lady in front of me noticed my whipcream and remembered she forgot hers, so she would not have to leave her baby in the basket to go back I gave her mine. And paid for the lady behind me, her avocados.

Selfless Acts Member Post

Left a note on the receipt for our waitress who did a great job. I hope it made her smile.

Selfless Acts Member Post

A table of women sitting next to us at a restaurant, one of them celebrating a milestone birthday, and I secretly asked their waiter to put their round of drinks on my tab...

Selfless Acts Member Post

Made a stranger smile.

Selfless Acts Member Post

I am beginning to understand that it actually is the little random Acts of Kindness that make the big difference. Yesterday, drinking my coffee on the way to work, I noticed a semi truck pulling up real close on my left side. First thought..."What the heck". And then I realized he had his right blinker on and NO one would let him in. I slowed way down. Let him in and noticed the person behind me did the same for the other semi trying to get in place. It's contagious!! Have a blessed day.

We are Family

"In every conceivable manner, the family is link to our past, bridge to our future." – Alex Haley

Selfless Acts Member Post
Convinced my father to agree to stop drinking liquor on weekdays. I thought I would start with those closest to me as a "warm up".

Selfless Acts Member Post
Took my Mom out to eat!

Selfless Acts Member Post
I let Jennifer have my car for the week so she could attend her boyfriend's graduation from Great Lakes Naval Academy on Saturday. She took it back to school last Sunday.

Selfless Acts Member Post
1 for today. I kinda hate counting it because it made me feel good! Family things are great!

Selfless Acts Member Post
Took my father-in-law out to an Opry show at the Ryman, thus crossing off an event on his Bucket List.

Selfless Acts Member Post

My husband LOVES football. My treadmill died yesterday. He got up off the football couch...Took me to Sears. And bought me an elliptical. Never complained once. Not once. He is back on couch now but missed some key plays. Gotta love him!

For the Children

"There can be no keener revelation of a society's soul than the way in which it treats its children." – Nelson Mandela

Selfless Acts Member Post

After another strong Thanksgiving celebration (we celebrated with my family yesterday and today), I took my nephew to the park and threw the football with him for an hour while everyone else sat inside at home watching TV. Happy kid who should sleep well on their 4-hour drive back to Atlanta tonight!

Selfless Acts Member Post

It was a small one, but while waiting at a redbox, gave the little girl sitting on the mechanical pony 50 cents to turn it on. Got a huge smile in return tho!

Selfless Acts Member Post

Good deed for my son...he agreed to give up an extra game station to a friend of mine so that she could give it to her boys for Christmas :)

Selfless Acts Member Post

I ran a 5K to benefit a preschool program in my town this week.

Selfless Acts Member Post

My nephew was attacked by a dog they had rescued so I made him chocolate chip cookies to make him feel better.

Selfless Acts Member Post

Took my son to the arcade last night and met up with a couple of his friends. With the tickets that they won, they all wanted to get "survivor bracelets" made of parachute rope. The youngest boy didn't have enough tickets to get a bracelet so my son shared his tickets and they were all able to get one :) wish I would have thought to get a picture of all the boys with their bracelets but here is my son with his :) <- proud mama!

Selfless Acts Member Post

I spent " Black Friday " buying Christmas presents for a foster child that is under privileged.

Selfless Acts Member Post

Working with a lady in another office to get her children's outgrown coats to children in need.

Selfless Acts Member Post

Helped at the 4K class. Took photos of all the kids for the teachers to make something nice for the parents. :)

Selfless Acts Member Post

5 today helping kids in the choir at the Purdue Christmas Show.

Selfless Acts Member Post

Bought some books for the underprivileged kids at the local school.

Selfless Acts`Member Post
Volunteering time at the Whitman Winterfest dishing out soup on behalf of Pack 22 Cub Scouts.

Selfless Acts Member Post
On a plane up to Oakland, while boarding I overheard a young girl maybe 7-8 years old upset that she had left her earphones home. They were headed to NY so long flight ahead. I gave her mine.

Selfless Acts Member Post
A little boy and his dad always come into my work. The little boy always wants "pizookie," but they never order one because it's too much for the two of them. So last night I made a small, kid-sized "pazookie" for them that we don't have on the menu. The little boy was so excited! It was the perfect size for him. :)

Selfless Acts Member Post
Our boys went to a daycare that had a high percentage of low income and aid supported clients, bought a bag full of hats and gloves and told them to give it out to anyone who needed some.

Selfless Acts Member Post
I donated to help an impoverished youth get a decent education. It's an opportunity for all of us to do one Selfless Act and contribute to a group that's providing educational opportunities to impoverished youth and helping build stronger communities.

Selfless Acts Member Post

I did three Selfless Acts this morning. Two guys from work were out of town on a field service job when I made breakfast for the shop on Tuesday morning. They heard I made breakfast while they were gone. So I surprised them both this morning with the same casseroles (smaller versions) that I made for the rest of the guys. They were very happy! Since I was up early making that I thought I would make breakfast for my son before he went off to high school. I surprised him with my special bowl of grits when he came downstairs. (his favorite thing I used to make him when he was a kid) I thought I saw a smile and may have heard a grunt from him. One never knows with a teenager! :-)

Selfless Acts Member Post

At our Girl Scout meeting tonight, we had planned to decorate Christmas cookies and then give them to people we looked up to in our lives. The girls decided to give their cookies to all of their current and former teachers, to the custodians, and to the office staff. With the help of the janitors, they were let into all of the classrooms and teacher's lounges to leave surprise thank you presents of handmade cookies and notes. :-)

College Kids Today, Our Future Tomorrow

"To do more for the world than the world does for you - that is success." – Henry Ford

Selfless Acts Member Post

So, we are "poor college students"... full time students, and we both have two jobs- in other words, we work hard for our money. Anyway, the other night at McDonald's we were waiting for our food that one of our best friends offered to by us (so we could get out of the house/library) and this man who was for sure in his 70s at least. He was so kind and had such a big smile on his face when he walked in. I got this feeling in the pit of my stomach that I should buy whatever he decided to order. So, I quickly slid my card through the machine and he responded with a shocked expression and a "no, no...you shouldn't have done that." When we were finished eating, my friends and I were walking towards the garbage can and the same sweet man handed us apple pies for "being so kind." This will be something I never forget.

Selfless Acts Member Post

As I was on my way to school, I saw a boy walking in the freezing cold. School was going to start in less than 10 minutes and from where he was, he wasn't going to make it. So I pulled over and got him. He thanked me over and over again. A start of a great day (:

Selfless Acts Member Post

Held the door open for a professor at school.

Selfless Acts Member Post

Came to campus with my roommate so she couldn't talk herself out of going to her 8 a.m. class. Even though I don't have class until 11, I got up at 7 am and am now sitting in the student union getting ahead on my homework because I have nothing else to do. As a 20 year old college student, waking up 4 hours before a class for someone else is beyond a Selfless Act (:

Selfless Acts Member Post

Every time I see Brian, Lisa, BK, Tom, Katie, Mike, and Sharon, I tend to enjoy life a little more and that usually lasts even after we have all gone back to our separate places in the country. The positive energy that flows from our group is contagious! While in Dallas, I wished that I could pick up one of our many tabs, but I knew that the guys probably wouldn't let me do it, no matter how many times I'd offer. So since I've been back, I've decided to pick up the smaller tabs (for a college students budget). :)

Selfless Acts Member Post

Again... Lauren and I true to reach out today. We went to get a couple new books at Barnes and Noble and we bought three children's books to donate to an organization that gives them to under privileged children for Christmas...We were proud to do it because we both absolutely love to read, so we feel like we're recruiting younger kids to love to read as well :)

Selfless Acts Member Post

Today a fella at the grocery store knocked down a bunch of glass jars full of spaghetti sauce. None of them broke. So Patrick and the three oldest kids helped him pick them all up! :)

Selfless Acts Member Post

Supported a school group by buying their lunch.

The Home of the Brave

"For those that will fight for it...FREEDOM ...has a flavor the protected shall never know." – Lance Corporal Edwin L. "Tim" Craft

Selfless Acts Member Post

Saw one of our young military men in line boarding a flight last night. He looked weary, so I asked were he had been. Looking me in the eye, he said he really couldn't say were he had been, but he knew where he was going. He was going home for the holidays. With a smile I gave him my first class seat and simply said thanks.

Selfless Acts Member Post

Tonight Mary and I wrote Christmas cards to injured soldiers who have come back from war to wish these heroes warmth and cheer while they recover over the holidays on American soil.

Selfless Acts Member Post

Clicked on a website to help feed homeless vets...

Selfless Acts Member Post

I wanted to share an organization that always need your support. If you have a military base or VA hospital in you region consider supporting Fisher House. Gift cards to grocery stores and local restaurants are appreciated, gas cards too. If you have time, volunteer.

Selfless Acts Member Post

Yesterday my Poms team applauded four soldiers as they entered the basketball arena where we were performing at half-time. Then at the end, the National Guard in charge of giveaways handed us a whole box of water bottles because we were so appreciative of them.

Friends in Need? Friends Indeed!

"The friend who can be silent with us in a moment of despair or confusion, who can stay with us in an hour of grief and bereavement, who can tolerate not knowing... not healing, not curing... that is a friend who cares". –
Henri Nouwen

Selfless Acts Member Post

2-hr drive to pick up a friend's child from grade school so she can help move her dad home with hospice for his last days fighting stage 4 lung cancer.

Selfless Acts Member Post

Drove a friend home from my 20th reunion this weekend as she was unable to do so herself ;)

Selfless Acts Member Post

Gave a friend that is out of work some money to buy groceries.

Selfless Acts Member Post

I put my own feelings aside in order to make a couple other people happy. And that, in turn, makes me happy. Funny how that happens.

Selfless Acts Member Post

Instead of returning something I bought for myself, I gave it to someone who will appreciate it more than me.

Selfless Acts Member Post

Made Sharon walk around the hospital so she can get well and get out... Sorry Sharon don't be mad but you must walk.

Selfless Acts Member Post

Spent the entire day helping a friend pack and move. I'm really beat, but it did feel good to pay that one forward since I've received that type of help before.

Selfless Acts Member Post

Lauren and I helped a friend jump start their car :)

Selfless Acts Member Post

Well, I don't know if this counts, but I'm taking care of my poor roommate who has the nasty stomach flu.

Taking Care, Taking Time

"Consciously or unconsciously, every one of us does render some service or other. If we cultivate the habit of doing this service deliberately, our desire for service will steadily grow stronger, and will make, not only our own happiness, but that of the world at large." - Mohandas Karamchand Gandhi

Selfless Acts Member Post
Visited a high school buddy's widow and children yesterday. He passed away in October from cancer. Just spent a little time with them.

Selfless Acts Member Post
For the past twenty days I've been helping my mom clean and organize her large home. The huge garage sale we had over the weekend provided multiple opportunities for Selfless Acts. People who were really in need got some incredible deals. :-) Now we get to donate LOTS of stuff!

Selfless Acts Member Post
Provided a friend with a truck, trailer and boxes to move with. Even spent several hours over 2 days moving boxes downstairs and loading them onto the trailer.

Selfless Acts Member Post
I helped my client finish a knitted blanket for her expected great grandchild, we have been making blankets and things for over a year.

Selfless Acts Member Post

My Co-Workers and I are spending the day at the Food Bank of the Rockies!

Selfless Acts Member Post

Every M-W & Th, I spend an hour in 2 different classrooms at the elementary school.

Selfless Acts Member Post

While we were in McKinney, TX this morning we were sitting outside of a coffee shop and a woman asked if we knew where Erwin St was. Rather than saying "I don't live here so I don't know" I asked what address she was looking for. She gave me the address and I launched the Navigation app on my phone and entered her destination. Then I read the directions while she jotted them down on a piece of paper. She was trying to meet friends at their church and was about to be late...pretty sure we got her there on time.

Selfless Acts Member Post

Talked to my cashier at the supermarket and made her laugh.

Selfless Acts Member Post

Helped a Mom & Grandma pick out some cool Skylanders for someone they love. Since my boys have taught me what's cool now-a-days, I figured I should pass it along. :)

Selfless Acts Member Post

There's a guy at Dunkin Donuts drive through who is one of the friendliest people I've met. I've never talked to him but every morning I go by his smile, the way he says "Hey buddy" and overall friendliness makes my day. I'm sure he deals with his fair share of grumpy people who haven't had their morning cup of joe. This morning I took some extra time to just say "Thank you. Your demeanor gives me a great start to the day and I look forward to getting my coffee here." I'm not sure if it counts as a Selfless Act but I think I made his day.

Selfless Acts Member Post

I helped a woman who wanted to give one pair of shoes to a young man...she ended up giving the entire family new clothes plus four boxes, FOUR BOXES of food and toiletry items for this suffering family. It was such a blessing to help get things to this family in need!

Selfless Acts Member Post

I have been tutoring a friend in College Algebra 2 nights a week since Sept. She didn't have any algebra in high school as she came from South Africa and their curriculum was quite different. Let's just say she is not a fan of math. Her final is coming up on the 18th. Pray for us! :)

Selfless Acts Member Post

Donated my time to united way for charity to help the homeless yesterday, was an awesome event!

Selfless Acts Member Post

A lady came in to our store today as a first time customer! She had been struggling losing her baby weight and needed to find a outfit for her Christmas party. After talking with her for awhile, I showed her a few outfits and put her in a fitting room! 40 minutes went by and she was continuously getting discouraged because nothing was fitting right and her self esteem was sinking. I wasn't going to give up! I continued bringing her outfits and finally the last one she tried on....she looked and felt amazing for the first time in years! The smile on her face was priceless. After getting undressed she came out of the fitting room in tears. She didn't realize how much it was going to cost her, and being a single mother (and with Christmas right around the corner) she simply couldn't afford the outfit. My heart sunk and I couldn't help but offer her my employee discount (50% off)! Again, her eyes watered up and she broke down crying saying no one has ever done anything like this for her before! She walked out not only with a new outfit, but with a newly found confidence!

Selfless Acts Member Post

I sat down and wrote four cards thanking Spoons Cafe, Cadillac Pizza Pub, Churchill's Pub, and The Grand Hotel for their amazing service this past weekend. All of those places made contributions to the weekend that I know some of us are going to consider one of the best of our lives. :)

Selfless Acts Member Post

Helped my brother clean his house after sitting empty for 7 years while going thru a long drawn out divorce. He uses his home to show for his business of building Earth shelter homes so we are all very happy he can start back showing his home and building again!!

Keeping it Neighborly

"When strangers start acting like neighbors... communities are reinvigorated." – Ralph Nader

Selfless Acts Member Post

Not sure what counts, but I had today off. Raining hard and garbage day. When the truck empties the 55 gallon recycling bins, the tops stay open. So I walked around the block after the truck left and closed all the lids to keep the water out.

Selfless Acts Member Post

Had our neighbor, retired bachelor, who's family is in Houston, and my sons friend, with no local family, and my daughters friend and 3 kids (recently divorced) all over for Thanksgiving. Not sure who enjoyed it more, us or them, so it might only count as a Selfless Act for us :)

Selfless Acts Member Post

Winterized a widowed neighbor's home & car for the winter.... Wrapped pipes, checked caulking and seals on doors & windows, checked anti-freeze in her car and the tire pressure. Went to Walmart twice, both times bought a cold beverage (Passionfruit-Mango green tea) for the clerk.

Selfless Acts Member Post

Made pumpkin bread and chocolate oatmeal cookies and brought them over to my neighbor along with a bouquet of fall flowers.

Selfless Acts Member Post
Walked and fed our neighbors dogs over Thanksgiving.

Selfless Acts Member Post
Picked up old newspapers and took stuff off of two neighbor's driveways and doors yesterday (and continuously) - one is only there once per month or so, and the other only during the holidays.

Selfless Acts Member Post
Updated our neighborhood contact list and put a copy in everyone's mailbox. As a volunteer fireman I feel like I do Selfless Acts everyday but I'm going to reach out beyond that. More to come.

Selfless Acts Member Post
Cleaned up after another person's dog in the alley behind my building.

Selfless Acts Member Post
Yesterday we got snow here, so went and shoveled the snow from the sidewalk in front of my neighbor's house.

Selfless Acts Member Post
Picked up a friend's paper in the driveway and hand delivered it to them at their door.

The Stories They Could Tell

"A test of a people is how it behaves toward the old. It is easy to love children. Even tyrants and dictators make a point of being fond of children. But the affection and care for the old, the incurable, the helpless are the true gold mines of a culture." – Abraham J. Heschel

Selfless Acts Member Post

Pulled into a Burger King lot to catch a call. I've been trying not to talk and drive. As I finished my call I saw an elderly couple in the lot rifling their pockets and purse and counting change. They looked pretty worried. I got out and approached them and asked if this was a good spot to eat. We chatted for a minute or two, just small talk to break the ice. I told them I was from out of town and hated to eat alone and asked if they would join me, my treat. After a couple of no's, and with my insistence they reluctantly agreed. This couple get the Selfless Act. Best time ever on the road.

Selfless Acts Member Post

Yesterday at my work a 90 year old man asked me if a nurse could tighten his back brace. I asked him if he knew he was in Pediatrics. It will take just a minute... He didnt want to go upstairs to adult care. First nurse I spoke with in adult care came down within 3 minutes. Took him in our well child room. Fixed his brace and off he went. He was born in 1922. Amazing compassionate nurse!!!

Selfless Acts Member Post
Helped my 74 year old neighbor in with his groceries.

Selfless Acts Member Post
Today I let several cars out of parking lots, etc and gave up a prime parking space up front for an older couple. Strange, but when you concentrate on doing nice things all of the time (and I would like to think that I do nice things quite often), nice things happen to you :) Pay it forward!

Selfless Acts Member Post
When I delivered mail, I gave time and my ears to a few of the elderly people who didn't have family.

Selfless Acts Member Post
Got a elderly lady's keys from her and brought her car around to the back door of the business she was leaving so as to greatly shorten her walk to her car.

Selfless Acts Member Post
Paid for the older couples flowers (poinsettias) with my bill and told the store clerk to tell them that it was covered after I left.

Selfless Acts Member Post
Saw an elderly woman in a wheelchair struggling to get her groceries from the cart to her car. I stopped and gave her a hand.

Selfless Acts Member Post

I had a birthday party for my Mom tonight & one of my friends that I have known pretty much all my life brings her Mom that has Alzheimer's, which is also my Mom's best friend, and she takes care of her, complimented me on my bracelet that I bought today shopping. I handed it to her and said I want you to have it for all you do!! The smile on her face was PRICELESS!!:)

Selfless Acts Member Post

I will visit individually, and entertain a group of 30 residents at a County Nursing Home on Friday night.

Selfless Acts Member Post

Put my $5 store cash coupon toward the old lady in front of me in the line at the grocery store.

All in a Day's Work

""The power of one man or one woman doing the right thing for the right reason, and at the right time, is the greatest influence in our society."" – Jack Kemp

Selfless Acts Member Post

At the last minute today at work just at quitting time one off coworkers was busy on a project and I stayed an extra while to help her finish so she could leave at a decent time.

Selfless Acts Member Post

Bought dinner for a girl at work who was feeling blue. Made her laugh.

Selfless Acts Member Post

We have a couple of college girls working for us through the holidays. One girl only has $5 in her account until she gets paid. I brought in food for her to take home and also stocked our fridge so while they are working they can eat and drink for free :-)

Selfless Acts Member Post

Got a call today from a client who does HVAC. One of their clients is a pediatric care center for drug addicted newborns. Their heat was out due to a computer switch malfunction and they have no IT guy. The computer couldn't turn on the heat. Got ahold of one of our techs and sent him to replace the switch. Call it Corporate Community Giving.

Selfless Acts Member Post
Stayed late at work to give someone a ride home.

Selfless Acts Member Post
Left a poinsettia plant anonymously on someone's desk.

Selfless Acts Member Post
Bought lunch for a co-worker.

Selfless Acts Member Post
Overheard a lady telling someone about her teenage son having a toothache and not having insurance nor the money to fix it since she recently lost her job. Being new to the area, she did not know a dentist either. Her son had the toothache for at least a week but did not tell his mother because he knew she did not have the money to pay for it. I called my dentist, explained the situation to him and told him to bill me. I gave the lady his phone number and told her to call my Dentist immediately, he was awaiting her call. She called and they told her she could work out a payment plan, and scheduled an appointment within the HOUR. They fixed the child's teeth yesterday afternoon. When she went to set up the payment plan, they told her it was already taken care of.

Selfless Acts Member Post
Arranged for a house cleaning to be done for a coworker whose son was injured recently and is living back at home while undergoing therapy.

Selfless Acts Member Post

Yesterday, I bought lunch for the sweet lady at the barber shop next door. She's always smiling and takes the time to stop and ask how I am so I chose to do this for her to let her know that I appreciate her positive attitude and kindness.

Selfless Acts Member Post

Taught someone something at work (finding revenue) and had her present it as her doings. She deserved it as she has been working so hard on this project. A good friend of mine told me (over 10 years ago) .. "It's amazing what you can accomplish when you don't care who gets the credit". Words to live by.

Selfless Acts Member Post

I'm staying an extra hour at work, even though its been a very long day, so my coworker can go home and be with her kids. I'm not excited about being on my feet for another hour, but I'm excited that I got another opportunity to do a deed :)

Selfless Acts Member Post

I surprised my co-workers with homemade breakfast casseroles right out of the oven. They were very happy and it was nice to see both of them devoured in all of 10 minutes. :-)

Selfless Acts Member Post

I found a job for two people this week. One started today as a medical assistant at a sports medicine clinic and and the other starts tomorrow at a consulting group.

Inspiration from Within

"At times our own light goes out and is rekindled by a spark from another person. Each of us has cause to think with deep gratitude of those who have lighted the flame within us." – Albert Schweitzer

Selfless Acts Member Post

Great idea. Hope I can live up to the group!! Thanks for the opportunity and for reminding me what my purpose is or should be in this life :)

Selfless Acts Member Post

Can I tell you how much I love this! Didn't realize I was in this group until now :-) tomorrow is a start to a new beginning involving Selfless Acts!!

Selfless Acts Member Post

I went to Wal-Mart to get some things for my mom. The man behind me only had one item, so I asked him to go ahead of me. He seemed so grateful. As I finished unloading the bags into the car, an older gentleman offered to take my cart (which is something I always do, but it was a first to be on the receiving end). I was kinda giddy as I left Wal-Mart.

Selfless Acts Member Post

Today, bring joy into the lives of others and you will bring it into your own life.

Selfless Acts Member Post

So there is this guy at work that wanted a drink. So I gave him a dollar for one. He got the drink and 2 came out of the machine so he gave one to someone else. :)

Selfless Acts Member Post

COMMENT: What a wonderful idea. We all do Selfless Acts daily but maybe don't realize until we start counting. People are good (as a whole) and how refreshing to be reminded. Thanks again.

Selfless Acts Member Post

Have a great Day everyone and notice the miracles, they are there.

Selfless Acts Member Post

Glad I found you

Selfless Acts Member Post

I had 2 extra bao from lunch and saw a homeless couple with a sign that read "Homeless and Hungry," so I offered them my food. They turned it down saying that they've tried them before and don't like them. I offered the bao to the next person asking for money, and he thanked me very graciously saying that he'd been hoping for food. If someone turns down your kindness, don't stop trying. Offer it to the very next person; they may be the one who needed it the most anyway.

Selfless Acts Member Post

The elderly lady I helped last night was on my return van back to the airport. After everyone is off and headed in I asked if she'd prefer a wheelchair. She watched my stuff, I went and got the wheelchair and took her all the way to the ticket counter. She said I was a very nice gentleman, thanked me for helping her last night again and said that I reminded her of her son. What a nice way to start the morning!

Selfless Acts Member Post

Bought the losing golf team a drink...parlayed that with buying two strangers a drink at a new restaurant. They couldn't stop shaking my hand, as if they won the lottery. What a great feeling.

Selfless Acts Member Post

Here's an idea. I know it applies to some of us. Introduce yourself to your neighbors and make sure they have a way to contact you in the event they need help. Sounds a little Mayberry, I know, but it still seems like something that we've lost that this group could help restore.

Selfless Acts Member Post

I like reading this page in the morning. Helps me get in the right frame of mind to start my day. Thanks everyone :-)

Selfless Acts Member Post

1 for today...new at this so am going to try harder tomorrow!!

Selfless Acts Member Post

I can't think of anything I did today. I worked at home and did not see anyone. I want to thank those of you who post your Selfless Acts. I like being inspired and I also like to steal your ideas. To those of you who don't post specifics, you inspire me too!! :)

Selfless Acts Member Post

Gave a fellow passenger my magazine to read on the plane and gave a homeless man a few bucks to eat. Plus 4 more small out of the routine gestures. Bottom line is I find myself looking for ways to be nice, but even better, I see more good that strangers are doing around me.

Selfless Acts Member Post

We are blessed just by knowing and being part of this site!

Selfless Acts Member Post

I like Mark's comment from earlier. I attended Franklin Covey training a few years ago. One thing I learned was See, Do, Get. As that approach relates to this group, if you can <u>See</u> a better world in your mind, you'll <u>Do</u> things to make it better and what you'll <u>Get</u> is a better world.

Selfless Acts Member Post

Proud of you ALL in the double digits! I JUST cannot keep up but I'm committed to making progress daily - getting others involved is even more FUN!! Loving THIS!

Selfless Acts Member Post

4 today. Wow, this feels good!

Selfless Acts Member Post

6 for me today...although a couple of them were responded to with bewilderment... The Berliners just don't quite know what to do with random kindness :-)

Selfless Acts Member Post

I saw this prayer at Pearl Harbor today and wanted to share it with this group....."Dear Lord, lest I continue my complacent way, help me to remember somehow out there a man died for me today. As long as there be war I then must ask and answer, am I worth dying for?".......this really made me think and it's a continued question I will ask of myself every day as long as our country is at war.

Selfless Acts Member Post

Let the lady behind me in line go ahead, while another gentleman paid a dollar towards the next 40 people's tabs. She paid it forward to me. Aren't doing deeds for other people fun?

Selfless Acts Member Post

I like to think that I always make kind gestures and those who know me, know that I want to work in nonprofit and I'm very big on volunteer work and donating. However, through this, I've realized that this has to be about doing things that I don't normally do.

Selfless Acts Member Post

So, because of my "series of unfortunate events" I've been unable to participate yet. But, I have been the recipient of Selfless Acts EVERYDAY since about 10 days ago. I can tell all of you good doers, keep up the good work. It's an incredible feeling when people reach out even in the smallest ways. No Selfless Act is too small!

Selfless Acts Member Post

I was so happy today! Been broke over the last week so haven't been to Starbucks. Got paid yesterday. Got my hair cut this morning and went to Starbucks afterward. I got up to the drive up window and told them I wanted to get the order behind me. The guy said, "wow, you're back, the last time you were in you started a chain reaction, the next 6 cars paid for the vehicle behind them!"

Selfless Acts Member Post

The work we started here is spreading! Just saw a post from a friend who is a Minister (not a member of this group) in St. Louis. He said he went into a doughnut shop this morning to get doughnuts for his Sunday school class and was told there was no charge. Apparently this morning, someone went in and gave them money and said to use it for following customers until it ran out. Awesome!

Selfless Acts Member Post

I read the first draft of the 1,000 Selfless Acts book. It is very motivating and inspiring. The Selfless Act posts and quotes included made me cry. Everyone did such wonderful Acts of Kindness and it makes me want to be a better neighbor, friend, wife, mother and daughter. I want to thank everyone and thank you Brian for assembling this fabulous group of people. Keep up the Selfless Acts. Remember a simple smile to a stranger can be contagious.

Homeless for the Holidays

"When a poor person dies of hunger, it has not happened because God did not take care of him or her. It has happened because neither you nor I wanted to give that person what he or she needed." – Mother Teresa

Selfless Acts Member Post

Tara, Jonah and I ate lunch at Rain Thai yesterday. We boxed up food to take home with us. As we turned off Hwy 27 to go to Green Life, a homeless couple stood at the corner of the off ramp and Manufacturers Rd holding a "Got Food?" sign. At Tara's suggestion, I rolled down the window and handed them the food with a smile.

Selfless Acts Member Post

Gave my sandwich to a homeless person and even tried to have a conversation with him...until the light changed to green :/

Selfless Acts Member Post

While in Montgomery on Sunday, I invited a homeless man into the Waffle House, sat him down at the counter and bought him a nice warm breakfast.

Selfless Acts Member Post

Coordinated a Blanket & Sleeping Bag Drive for my son's High School Hockey teams. We collected 333 total and delivered them to the Andre House (homeless shelter in downtown Phoenix).

Selfless Acts Member Post
Yesterday I gave some money to a homeless guy.

Selfless Acts Member Post
All my change from the center console to the homeless at a light plus the singles from my wallet.

Selfless Acts Member Post
Gave homeless person $5.

Selfless Acts Member Post
Gave money to a homeless person.

Selfless Acts Member Post
Gave a homeless woman and her dog a granola bar.

Selfless Acts Member Post
The world has less trash, 2 less hungry, and one interesting homeless dude who would not take money or food. He just wanted to talk to someone..... He said that he "smelled bad and was dirty so no one ever talks to me, I get lonely".

Selfless Acts Member Post
Bought a homeless guy a cup of coffee on Friday at the gas station.

Selfless Acts Member Post
2 for yesterday - fed the homeless at the Community Kitchen and then decided to stop and give blood:) Still have to spot the opportunities today:)

Selfless Acts Member Post

Most of my Selfless Acts have really been my wife before she was added to the group. She likes people more than I do and works in a hospital. LOL I build houses and don't run across too many people during the day. Last night after Jeff posted about a meeting with Brian she asked when my personality changed. I don't really think it has but she seems to think if I was once close friends with these thoughtful caring men, it must have. She called me at work to read the perspective post about the homeless and suggested I find something to do today. She had surgery a week ago and hasn't been out of the house. She volunteers at a food pantry; quite a while ago a co-volunteer gave her the idea to keep a book bag in her car. She fills them with water, snacks that won't melt or spoil and a Bible. She's added a blanket now that the weather is colder. I drove her car to work today and took a couple out of the trunk. Made a point to drive on a street there are usually homeless people at the stoplight. So chalk one up for me today.

Selfless Acts Member Post

Bought food for a lady asking for money outside of Walgreen's...Buffalo wings to be specific :)

Selfless Acts Member Post

I bought a woman asking for money a dinner.

Selfless Acts Member Post

I had some winter jackets in my car to take to Goodwill. Gave one to the homeless man at the grocery store. I stopped and asked if he had a warm jacket and he told me he didn't so we went out to my car and I let him have his pick. It was nice to walk together a little and talk. I'm sure most people just walk on by without even saying hello. I'm going to make an effort to talk to him from now on. He was very sweet.

Selfless Acts Member Post

I was shopping with my 15 yr. old daughter and she asked if we could go into Pease Candy shop so she could buy some caramel corn. It had special meaning to her because her grandma used to take her to buy it all the time & she had passed away 2 years ago. My daughter used her own money that she had just earned babysitting to buy a good-sized bag. As we were leaving we saw a homeless man sitting with a 'will work for food' sign up ahead. As we drew closer to the intersection my daughter asked me, 'mom, do you think it would be ok if I gave my caramel corn to the homeless man?' I was shocked & proud at the same time. When we got up next to him she rolled down her window and offered it to him. He said 'God bless you' & thanked her. She felt so good & so did I. We then went around the corner to Wendy's and ordered him 2 hamburgers & took them to him. He was so grateful & I felt so proud of my daughter.

Pets Are People Too

"Pets are humanizing. They remind us we have an obligation and responsibility to preserve and nurture and care for all life." – James Cromwell

Selfless Acts Member Post
Came across a dog that lost his parents today. I was able to contact them off the dog collar and get him home!!

Selfless Acts Member Post
Turned the car around and tracked a lost dog running by the road last night around mid-night, it looked lost and freaked out.

Selfless Acts Member Post
I HELP DOGS LIVE. BUT I DON'T HAVE TIME TO LIST ALL OF MY ENDEAVORS...TOO BUSY DOING GOOD DOGGIE DEEDS!!!! :-)

Selfless Acts Member Post
While out on a walk last night with my hubby, two beautiful (well groomed) dogs were running around near a heavy traffic street (Carefree Highway). We were able to get them to come to us and luckily one had a tag with a phone number. We called the owner who lived 2 miles away (to think they didn't get hit is a miracle). We sat with the dogs on the edge of the street petting them until he showed up with his son. They had tears in their eyes (and so did I). They were so thankful the dogs were okay.

Selfless Acts Member Post

Lauren and I signed up to volunteer at the pet shelter on Wednesday for a couple hours.

Selfless Acts Member Post

Babysitting Violet, the pit-less bull, while her momma out of town.

Selfless Acts Member Post

I donated money to an animal shelter.

Selfless Acts Member Post

Adopted a puppy today at Canine Assistants.

Selfless Acts Member Post

Drove across town to pick up a donation box for a local animal shelter so it can be placed in my friend's store.

'Tis the Season

"My idea of Christmas, whether old-fashioned or modern, is very simple: loving others. Come to think of it, why do we have to wait for Christmas to do that?" – Bob Hope

Selfless Acts Member Post

Yesterday I was in Target shopping for a Christmas tree that was on sale. An elderly lady was trying to pull these heavy boxes off the shelf so I went over and helped her pull down the tree she wanted and help her load it into her cart. Turns out she got the last one and it was the same one I wanted. She offered to let me have it and I told her to take it and have a very Merry Christmas! :)

Selfless Acts Member Post

Our family Christmas tradition is for $50 Pollyanna gift exchange. This year we are forgoing the gift exchange for a family donation ($1000) to Hurricane Sandy relief fund.

Selfless Acts Member Post

Selected three families to send special anonymous cash gifts to brighten their Christmas seasons.

Selfless Acts Member Post

Planning our office Christmas events & we've all decided to donate to the local toy drive instead of giving to each other.....this staff is all new within the last 4 months and working together to help others. I KNOW I hired the right group!

Selfless Acts Member Post

Took a group of Girl Scouts to a Christmas show.

Selfless Acts Member Post

Just picked my Christmas Angel from the Angel tree at work. Buying kitty and puppy toys for the Animal Shelter my company is supporting.

Selfless Acts Member Post

Picked not 1 but 2 angels off the angel tree at the mall last night -- a 6-year-old girl (Ayla's age; she wants a toy kitchen) and a 49-year-old homeless man who needs a sleeping bag. I'm happy to give it to him.

Selfless Acts Member Post

Instead of giving members of my family a token Xmas gift this year, I've made a sizable (for me) donation on their behalf to a relief organization comprised of volunteer veterans and medical personnel who are assisting with recovery efforts in the wake of Hurricane Sandy. Much of what I knew growing up on the Jersey shore was destroyed and I still have friends and family there who have been, and still are affected, so thought it was a much more meaningful way to say Merry Xmas.

Selfless Acts Member Post

Sent 2 shoeboxes of goodies for a girl and boy with "Operation Christmas Child". Both for a 12-14 year old. Don't know what part of the world they will end up but prayed over them and dropped them off.

Selfless Acts Member Post

I bought a Christmas tree for a family in need and donated toys for her daughter for Christmas.

Selfless Acts Member Post

We are donating diapers and wipes to our apartment complex's sharing Christmas tree for a 6 month old boy named Eyan :)

Selfless Acts Member Post

Tonight my roommate and I let some balloons go outside. They weren't for anyone we know but we wrote some messages that had Christmas Spirit in them. We sent them up for a person who needed a miracle.

Selfless Acts Member Post

Teamed up with my in-laws and supported a family for Christmas, a single mom and four little kids. We had such a great time playing Santa. Definitely one of the most rewarding things I've done in a while.

Selfless Acts Member Post

Tom and I have decided to "donate Christmas" this year. We plan to take the money we would have spent on each other and others and select several families from the giving tree and make their Christmas a happy one. We encourage everyone to go to their local giving tree and help a family out this year.

Selfless Acts Member Post

One of my friends at work lost her mother 2 years ago. Then she lost her mother in law. Then her family had some difficult times. Her mother always made Christmas so special for her and her son. A group of us including a doctor pulled together and made sure her and her son will have a special Christmas. We celebrated tonight by coming together. Pretending it was a birthday celebration and gave her some money to make Christmas bright! It's her mom coming through us. I firmly believe that. Tis the time...

Selfless Acts Member Post

I have been really stressing about what to get my co-workers for Christmas. What do you get people who are blessed with the love of family and friends? With inspiration from this website I have decided to donate the money I was going to spend for gifts. So this morning I went and selected all the remaining angel tree tags for the Friends for Life charity. I strongly suggest they do the same. Instead of buying gifts none of us really needs please spend the money on your favorite charity.

Selfless Acts Member Post

Mary and I donated to toys for tots today.

Selfless Acts Member Post

Today, Lauren and I gave to the Salvation Army along with wrapping and giving our sharing tree gift. We also brought gifts, a gingerbread house kit and other crafts to a couple boys we babysit yesterday. These past couple days have truly warmed our hearts in this freezing winter, Minnesotan weather :)

Selfless Acts Member Post

Yesterday I purchased 5 outfits, gloves and hats for 5 children from the angel tree at a local middle school in Franklin TN. I have learned that a lot of these families live in run down trailers and some with no running water. Thank you, Tamara, for giving me the idea to buy gifts for the less fortunate in the name of co-workers and family that we would have otherwise purchased gifts for. Thank you Dana for letting me know about these children.

The Winner's Purse

"Fame is a vapor, popularity an accident, and riches take wings. Only one thing endures and that is character." – *Horace Greeley*

Selfless Acts Member Post

My wife and I were heading into the grocery store. I spotted a loose cart and told her if she collected it and put it away that it'd be a Selfless Act. She got it and, believe it or not, the woman who'd used the cart before had forgotten her purse in it. Lisa turned the purse into the store manager...2 deeds for the price of 1!!!

Selfless Acts Member Post

Today I was doing some shopping and stopped for a quick lunch and as I was leaving the restaurant I noticed the van beside me had its sliding door open and a purse and packages could be seen. I went back into the restaurant and asked these 2 women if they by chance were driving this van. They replied they were & the one lady jumped up and said oh my purse is in there. She came out and shut the door and thanked me and said thank God there are still honest people in this world!:)

The More I Listen, the More I Hear...The More I Look, the More I See

"Truth is not something outside to be discovered, it is something inside to be realized." - Osho

Selfless Acts Member Post

Got stuck finishing up the book I am working on and went for a drive to clear my head as I tend to do. I ended up in the middle of nowhere Texas and was just about to turn around when I saw a woman next to her car looking very pissed off. She had a flat and a spare but no jack evidently and had been waiting for her husband for a half hour. He drove up just as I finished changing her tire :)

Selfless Acts Member Post

I was on my way into a grocery store when I stopped to let an elderly man go in front of me. As I followed behind him, once in the store he stops and turned and said "thank you"...now I thought it was for letting him thru the door first, then he said "...for the smile". Selfless Acts do not have to cost money nor come from great thought or detail. Sometimes a simple smile can make a huge difference in someone's life. So honored to be a part of this event and know together we can make a difference.

Selfless Acts Member Post

Every time I took my father-in-law anywhere the 10 days he was here, I put on his favorite XM channel instead of mine.

Selfless Acts Member Post

Sent diapers to two much needed and deserved new parents.

Selfless Acts Member Post

Supported small business Saturday and shopped locally yesterday.

Selfless Acts Member Post

I picked up litter while walking to the beach this morning. I should bring a bag with me next time!

Selfless Acts Member Post

Today on a long 4 hour flight there came a request from the attendants for any medical personnel on the flight to assist with a medical emergency. As a Registered Respiratory Therapist this catches my attention, but I will defer to a Physician on board. A minute later, there came a second call. This prompted my getting up and going back to assess the situation. There was an elderly lady on the floor in the aisle, out for the count. Long story short, she was in pretty bad shape and with minimal medical equipment I was able to stabilize her and get her to St Louis. The back story here was her husband just lost his sister and they were headed to her funeral. I am sure that I was meant to be there so he wouldn't have two losses. Not so much a Selfless Act, but doing what I was supposed to do.

Selfless Acts Member Post

Helped a teenager push his car out of the right hand lane on the off-ramp this evening.

Selfless Acts Member Post

My 13 yr. old son had a fund raiser for his basketball team. They were selling these plastic cards that had a list of "deals" and savings off of different restaurants, stores, etc. Instead of going door to door or bring to work, I just bought them and am them giving away. Helped the school and random people that could use a good deal!

Selfless Acts Member Post

Started off the day with a fun one. In case you missed it in my profile pic, I have a thing for cycling. On my usual Pecos Road ride in the bike lane was a huge 100 foot or so stretch of broken glass mirror. Lots and lots of shattered glass. Nasty..... Bikers would have to swing out on a pretty busy road to miss it. Dangerous.....So I went back post ride and cleaned it all off. Very cool part was that every biker riding by thanked me. Made the effort feel appreciated. Kudos to my lovely wife Irene for driving the sag wagon with flashing lights to keep me safe. I guess that counts as two!

Selfless Acts Member Post

Helped someone adjust their car in the parking lot at work so they wouldn't knock down a string of motorcycles.

Selfless Acts Member Post

Gave up my seat on the first shuttle bus to the hotel for the mom and baby. Gave up my seat on the second shuttle bus to the hotel for an elderly lady.

Selfless Acts Member Post

Donated blood today for the first time ever.

Selfless Acts Member Post

I cut out coupons and placed them by products in the store. I'll plan on doing that one another day. It was kinda like giving out money.

Selfless Acts Member Post

On the way out of the Post Office, picked up a lost letter in the street and returned it to the Post Office.

Selfless Acts Member Post

Stopped on my way home and helped a stranded motorist change a flat tire. Even though I probably ruined a good pair of khakis, the guy was much appreciative as he was having a hard time loosening a couple of the lug nuts and I was able to break them loose.

Selfless Acts Member Post

Picked up trash when I saw it and threw it away.

Selfless Acts Member Post

A disabled man was driving the motorized cart at Target to his car, leaving his motorized cart not knowing what to do with it....I took it back in the Target for him.

Selfless Acts Member Post

Picked up a piece of trash thrown on the floor in the lobby of my apartment building.

Selfless Acts Member Post

Gave up a sweet parking spot at Costco so that the person behind me could have it.

Selfless Acts Member Post

Ordered a sausage dog at a lunch counter yesterday. Just as I heard the lady next to me order a sausage dog, I heard the cook say that "my" sausage dog was the last one until the delivery truck arrived. I quickly changed my order so the lady next to me could have "her" sausage dog.

Selfless Acts Member Post

I found a credit card and called and reported it to the credit card company.

Selfless Acts Member Post

I picked up garbage around my subdivision on my daily 4 mile walk :)

Selfless Acts Member Post

Called and got help for someone on the roadside who was in trouble.

A Whole "Latte" Goodness

"No kind action ever stops with itself. One kind action leads to another. Good example is followed. A single Act of Kindness throws out roots in all directions, and the roots spring up and make new trees. The greatest work that kindness does to others is that it makes them kind themselves." – Amelia Earhart

Selfless Acts Member Post

Paid for the car behind me at McDonalds...Happy Monday :)

Selfless Acts Member Post

I posted this on the community bulletin board in our neighborhood. Hopefully the second person in line gets theirs too. "Here's a $10 gift card for two cups of coffee...one cup for you and one cup for the person in line behind you. PAY IT FORWARD!

Selfless Acts Member Post

Finally got to pay for the person behind me at Starbucks!

Selfless Acts Member Post

I bought my friend at work a coffee card because she offered to work for me on a Saturday so I can go see my mother who lives alone and takes care of my brother who rescues strays.....3 for 1.

Selfless Acts Member Post

Bought the person's coffee behind me.

Selfless Acts Member Post

Just took advice from here and paid it forward at Starbucks!

Selfless Acts Member Post

Just paid for a woman's coffee at McDonalds. Happy Friday (:

Selfless Acts Member Post

Paid for the person's order in the car behind me at Starbucks. Small gestures add up. Keep it going!

Selfless Acts Member Post

Monday thru Friday while stopping at Dunkin Donuts for my morning coffee, I bought the person behind me their coffee.

This morning, I made my routine stop at the Dutch Brothers drive-thru and the couple in the car behind me appeared to be in a heated argument. Hands were flying - kind of like what happens when BK irritates me when he can't keep his hands off the stereo, ;) but only worse... So when I got to the window, I paid for my coffee then handed the guy $20 and told him I'd like to pay for the car behind me and whatever was left was a tip, but to tell the couple to pass it on. I only hope their arguing ceased.

Selfless Acts Member Post

Surprised someone I didn't know in the breakfast line when I just paid for her breakfast. She appeared to be in shock:) LOL

Selfless Acts Member Post

This morning, I passed on my full stamp card that's good for a free coffee to the car behind me. This will become routine. :)

Keep the Change

"God gave you a gift of 86 400 seconds today. Have you used one to say thank you" – William Arthur Ward

Selfless Acts Member Post

Had lunch with my good friend Marcia to celebrate her birthday. We were college roommates at Sangamon State (now UIS) 30 years ago then worked together at SIUMED for 10 years and had lunch together at least weekly. For an hour today, we laughed, reminisced and laughed some more and then ended the lunch leaving a $10 tip on our $20 meal.

Selfless Acts Member Post

I got a haircut and, based on our conversation, learned that the girl cutting my hair was a little down on her luck. I gave her my debit card to pay but forgot I had a 2-dollar off coupon from giving to a charity a few weeks back. When I remembered, she offered to re-run the card and I told her to forget about it and that I'd use the coupon next time. She asked if I was sure and I said yes, wrote in a nice tip and went to my car. Then I thought I should have paid that coupon forward to the person behind me. I caught up with the girl before she seated the next customer and asked her to give the coupon to them when she'd finished cutting their hair. I figured if it came from her that maybe they'd put the $2 back in her tip.

Selfless Acts Member Post

I tipped our shuttle driver $10 bucks. Yes, I was the only one.

Selfless Acts Member Post

Gave a waitress an extra special tip with a hand written note. I hope it made her have a great day.

Selfless Acts Member Post

Left a 20% tip on top of the 18% gratuity that was already on the bill...ok I didn't realize there was already a gratuity added until after I told the server to keep the change...but once I realized...I decided to leave the tip as is :)

Selfless Acts Member Post

Took a Christmas card, dropped a few lines of thanks and a nice tip for the housekeeping crew at each hotel we stayed in over the long weekend.

Selfless Acts Member Post

Went out to eat and gave the waiter a $10 tip on a $22 bill.

The DoNation

"We make a living by what we get. We make a life by what we give." – Winston S. Churchill

Selfless Acts Member Post

I have been working on this one since August. In June, a coworker and good friend's wife was involved in a critical car accident. With a traumatic brain injury and a slim chance of survival, somehow she pulled through. But she was on life support for a week, 4 weeks in ICU and almost 2 full months in the hospital. The hospital bills became insurmountable. On the verge of having to file for bankruptcy, his parents sold their house in Connecticut to move down and help him, not only to take care of his wife, but to help with the bills. I wanted to do something to help out as well. Behind the scenes I organized 2 golf tournaments to raise money, and a couple other Departments joined in and helped raise money for this cause through auctions. All together we raised $1,360. Today at the end of our Christmas Conference we were going to present him with the check. My CEO called me into his office first thing this morning and handed me a check matching what we had raised. So we were able to present him with $2,760 today to help with Christmas for his 3 kids and to help pay some bills. It was definitely one of those feel good moments. His wife still has a long way to go but making progress every day!

Selfless Acts Member Post

My roommate and I cleaned out every closet and storage bin we have today and we're donating the clothes we love but don't wear, some jackets, and extra misc. material things to the Salvation Army/red cross tomorrow.

Selfless Acts Member Post

Donated bags of kid's clothes to the Red Cross today.

Selfless Acts Member Post

I surprised the Salvation Army Bell Ringer with a $100 donation.

Selfless Acts Member Post

Dropped the last dollar from my wallet in a Salvation Army kettle today.

Selfless Acts Member Post

On Thanksgiving, cooked and gave away 5 turkeys to those without...

Selfless Acts Member Post

Yesterday at the grocery store I made a donation that will feed 70 families this holiday season.

Selfless Acts Member Post

Donated to the Salvation Army and gave tribute to a man who recently passed away by buying a piece of his art to remember his past kindness.

Selfless Acts Member Post
Does it count the countless donations to the Salvation Army bell ringers??? If so mark me down for ummm ???

Selfless Acts Member Post
I donated 3 dollars to Saint Jude's. On a tight budget that was the best I could do :)

Selfless Acts Member Post
I left my quarter in my cart at Aldi today so that someone had a free cart rental.

Selfless Acts Member Post
We had an entertainment center that I had put on Craigslist. Had some interest for it for $400 but we decided instead to donate it to the Salvation Army. Took it off Craigslist. Hope someone enjoys it!

Selfless Acts Member Post
Did the round up on all my shopping bills for the change charities.

Selfless Acts Member Post
I purchased food items to donate.

Selfless Acts Member Post
Donated a bag of clothes to a guy working at the McDonalds drive thru (yes...I go there often) for a clothing drive he was having :)

Selfless Acts Member Post

I'm getting off to a slow start but today we bought a bag of groceries for the needy.

Conclusion

At the beginning of the book I wrote about how I questioned the life I had led. I wrote about how I questioned my legacy. I am not at all saying that what we've started here is done...I think there is a lifetime of good to be done and I am personally motivated to do as much as I can. But because of Scott's simple challenge to "do for others", I am sure of the life I will live going forward and I am sure of the legacy that will build as a result of that life.

When I started the 1,000 Selfless Act challenge I thought those who would join the group and contribute to the cause would be the ones giving kindness and making others feel better. I honestly failed to comprehend the impact the challenge would have on those doing the Selfless Acts. I'll share some of their feedback a little later on in this chapter.

I am sure there is some official psychological definition to what happened to me and others as a result of this challenge. I went from being apprehensive, to seeing that apprehension in others, to watching the group's members let their guards down, to witnessing and hearing of the transformation they went through in the process.

This challenge ultimately became an amazing journey that many people who'd never even met took together over the holiday season in 2012. If you think about it, at the time of this writing, our 1,000 Selfless Acts challenge didn't even exist 60 days ago. Given all that was done and all of those who benefited I'd say we definitely defined the moment.

The 1,000 Selfless Acts group members agreed to allow me to write this book. We will use money made from this project to continue to pay it forward and to continue to make whatever difference we can as a direct result of those first 1,000 Selfless Acts. Whatever that adds up to will likely be a part of our legacy and, in a small way, part of what we are remembered for throughout the rest of our lives.

Over the years I have learned to value different opinions and viewpoints, though I hardly believe that when it comes to the most controversial issues we can all be right, all of the time. I doubt seriously any of us will see a single government or a single religion that brings us all together. Each of us will ultimately decide what kind of world we are going to live in and it is up to us as individuals to take action and make this world a better place.

I'd like to encourage you to ask yourself a few questions. How do others see you? How do your children see you? What will your grandchildren know about you? Will a lifetime of moments define you, or will you seize the moments and define your life? Whose lives will you change or make better in the process of living your own?

If each of us live to be 75 years old and there are 365 days in a year, then we each have 27,375 days...not a day more. The math is the same regardless of the color of our skin; whether we are rich or poor, tall or short, male or female. How much time do you have left? If it all ended tomorrow, what would your legacy be?

In the Appendix of this book you will find a step-by-step guide, or recipe, to create your own movement that can lead to a better world.

As you consider whether or not to take action, you should understand that not everyone will buy into your cause. Some will question your motives while others dismiss your challenge and say they already do more good in the world than bad. I urge you to lean on those people to help you build momentum and set an example for those who don't readily go out of their way for others. That's probably the one regret I have taken from this...that I didn't have a good response to those who dismissed our challenge because they felt they already make the world a better place. Those are exactly the kind of people you need to help you to set a good example for those who don't instinctively consider and care for others.

The Marines teach leadership as "the sum of those qualities of human understanding, moral character and intellect that allow you to inspire and control a group of people". If you are to accept this challenge as your own, then you are going to have to lead your group...keep them informed, keep them motivated. It's a small price to pay for the good that will come of it.

I'd like to thank you for reading our story and to wish you the best of luck in the future!

At the beginning of this chapter I wrote that I would share some of the feedback I received from those who participated in the 1,000 Selfless Acts challenge. I also said that I was surprised, and humbled, by the impact the challenge on the members of our group. Here is some of that feedback:

Group Member Feedback

"For me personally, I read your initial post and Irene let me respond on her Facebook that I was "in", with a caveat. I would have to get my own Facebook page if I seriously wanted to participate. This was not an easy thing for me to do as I am pathologically private from a social networking perspective. I was, however drawn to the concept viscerally. I just have a core belief that good begets good, Karma, whatever.

As I began my personal journey, I too struggled with the idea that through posting, the deeds could become ego driven. Man was I wrong. The whole idea that through sharing we foster good became central to my whole process. You hit the nail in the head with your suggestion that by posting we share ideas, help each other to learn and see there are many, many ways to do "Selfless Acts".

My transition became one of wanting to promote kindness, to one of seeking an opportunity to serve others, to seeing and feeling the good that is there when you open your eyes and heart. By the way, seeing and feeling the good is not a passive event. What I discovered is that the window to seeing kindness is by being kind."

Group Member Feedback

"Thank you for bringing this group together. I find myself counting on it to be part of my day now."

Group Member Feedback

"Thank you for the challenge that you proposed in creating this group. Personally, it was very difficult for me to post Selfless Acts. Actually, I probably posted less than one in 10 that actually were accomplished. I believe that most of the group members were the same way. The actual number of Selfless Acts achieved by this group most likely numbered into several thousands, if not, tens of thousands."

Group Member Feedback

"I think the Selfless Acts group is bringing out my sentimental side (not that I need much help with that). When I think about how I was raised, many of my memories are from when our families were together. Now, as an adult, it's so cool to see how many people this is influencing to be better people. I just want to say how much I truly appreciate all that's been done to coordinate this!"

Group Member Feedback

"Some people think they can't make a difference in the world. This group proved otherwise, and the things people did are simple to do. Anyone can do them, and it doesn't always have to take money or a huge amount of time."

Group Member Feedback

"Thanks to all that took the time to make the world a better place to inhabit. I for one am a better person, or at least try to be, because one person took the time to focus my energy on the good that can be if we let it shine through."

Group Member Feedback

"Thank you for making us more aware of our surroundings and more aware that we can do more for mankind. Super-great people doing Selfless Acts is an awesome thing to watch and be a part of."

Group Member Feedback

"I think the group was a complete success based upon your initial post and I would like to congratulate you and thank you for the group. I have always considered myself charitable and generous in pretty much an anonymous fashion (and those are traits that I don't go around beating my chest about), but you have certainly brought out the best in me this holiday season. It is easy to get caught up in your own personal problems and forget that there are many, many people worse off than you or I could ever dream about. I think that you and several people in the group opened my eyes to even more possibilities of charitable ways or Selfless Acts that I will always carry with me and will continue to "pay-it-forward" on a daily basis with a much greater awareness now!

I do agree that the group really has become bigger than each and every one of us and has really taken on its own life form. Regardless of what you decide to do with the group, it will live on the hearts and souls of all who have been exposed to every Selfless Act and comment posted."

Group Member Feedback

"I just want to say thanks for this idea and letting me be a part of it. It's been fun reading what others are doing and getting inspired by all. It would be great to have a place to go like 1,000 Acts for encouragement as well as to share the fun deeds but understand it could take on a life of its own keeping it all going. I want to let you know whatever the future is for 1,000 Acts and whatever may be needed for its future, I am offering my support."

Appendix A – The Recipe

Steps to setup a 1,000 Selfless Acts or Acts of Kindness Group:

1. Send a message, similar to mine in Chapter 4 – The Challenge. Let them know to hit "Like" on your message to opt in. Wait a week or so to see who has accepted your challenge.

2. Create a Group in Facebook and name it whatever you like. You can do this from your Home page, on the left hand column "Create Group".

3. After you've created the group you can click on it in Facebook. You can set the Group settings to your preferences. Options include whether you will allow anyone in the Group to invite others or if you have to approve them first. You can also adjust the Group settings to allow anyone in the Group to post to it and whether or not anyone outside of the Group can see the posts. That is all a matter of personal preference.

4. I created a file with instructions on how to post to the group and posted that file to the Group. This gave me an idea as to who was actively participating in the group. FYI, Facebook allows you to see who has read the Group posts, but not after you reach 100 Group members. This is a privacy setting that you cannot override.

5. I let the group know that I would post an update every couple of days and that the update would

include a count of Good Deeds and Acts of Kindness committed. As the Group and the number of Acts grew and gained momentum, I posted a nightly update at 10PM my time. This gave the group a Home Base that they could return to every night or every morning to see where we stood. You can "Pin" that post to the Group page by clicking on the upper right-hand corner of that post. This keeps the last count from scrolling off of the top of the page as others post their updates. Remember to unpin the previous post when you create the next day's update.

6. I read every single post, and commented or "Liked" to ensure the Group member that posted knew I had seen their post. Remember, as the group grows you are going to have people join that you may not know. Try to make them feel welcome from their first post...they may end up being your most active Group member.

7. Try not to judge the posts. Some people are more humble than others, some people are more awkward initially as they get started focusing on others. There is no right answer when a person's heart is in the right place.

8. It's possible that not everyone is going to agree with your approach or the forum of the Group. I reserved the right to "Block" people from the group and to "Remove" derogatory comments that might be posted. The last thing you want is a

114

philosophical argument breaking out on a site that is designed to make the world a better place. Let them setup their own Group and they can argue their lives away if they want.

9. Have fun! You are going to find that doing good for others makes you feel good. Embrace that...I am certain it is not an accident and that it is supposed to work that way.

Made in the USA
Lexington, KY
02 May 2013